BREAD

Dorothy Turner

Illustrations by John Yates

Carolrhoda Books, Inc./Minneapolis

All words that appear in **bold** are
explained in the glossary on page 30.

First published in the U.S. in 1989 by
Carolrhoda Books, Inc.

LIBRARY OF CONGRESS
Library of Congress Cataloging-in-Publication Data

Turner, Dorothy
   Bread / Dorothy Turner ; illustrated by John Yates.
      p.   cm.
   Bibliography: p.
   Includes index.
   Summary: Describes how bread is produced, prepared, and eaten and
presents some background history, as well as two recipes.
   ISBN 0-87614-359-1 (lib. bdg.)
   1. Bread—Juvenile literature. 2. Bread industry—Juvenile
literature. [1. Bread.] I. Yates, John, ill. II. Title.
   TX394.T87   1989
   664'.7523—dc19
                                                        88-23630
                                                            CIP
                                                            AC

Printed in Italy by G. Canale C.S.p.A., Turin
Bound in the United States of America

1 2 3 4 5 6 7 8 9 10 99 98 97 96 95 94 93 92 91 90 89

Contents

Bread around the world. 4

The history of bread. 6

Bread made from wheat. 10

Leavened and unleavened bread. 12

Bread as food. 14

Bread from a bakery. 16

Bread from a factory. 20

Beliefs about bread. 22

A recipe for whole wheat bread. 26

A recipe for chappatis. 29

Glossary. 30

Index. 32

Bread around the world

There is one food that is eaten in more places and in greater amounts than any other. That food is bread. When you think of bread, you probably picture a plump, crusty loaf. But bread comes in all shapes and sizes. It can be long and skinny,

short and round, or flat enough to roll up.

The bread from one country can be quite different than the bread from another. The Soviet Union is known for its hearty loaves of Russian rye. Round, heavy pieces of bread called **chappatis** are popular in India. In Mexico, **tortillas**, a thin, flat bread made from corn, are found at almost every meal. Flat or thin, soft or hard, bread is an important food all over the world.

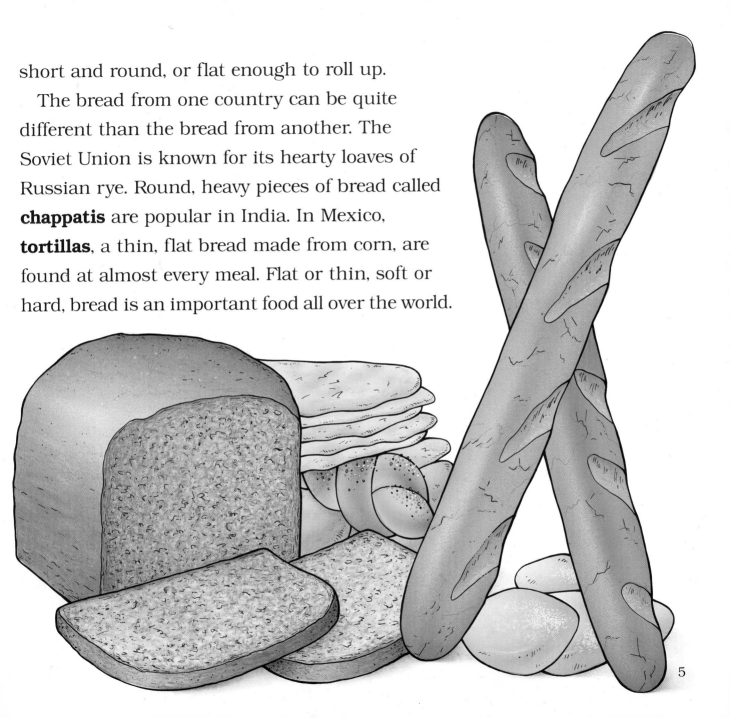

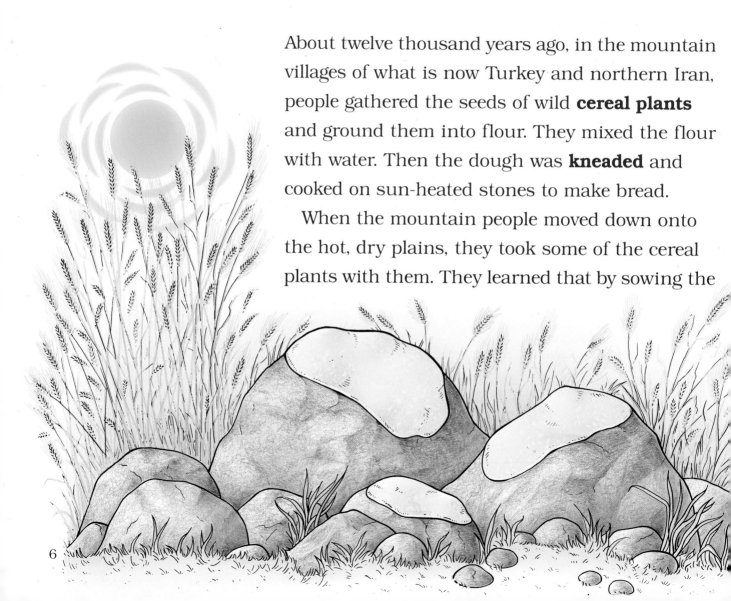

The history of bread

About twelve thousand years ago, in the mountain villages of what is now Turkey and northern Iran, people gathered the seeds of wild **cereal plants** and ground them into flour. They mixed the flour with water. Then the dough was **kneaded** and cooked on sun-heated stones to make bread.

When the mountain people moved down onto the hot, dry plains, they took some of the cereal plants with them. They learned that by sowing the

Right: This ancient Egyptian wall painting, which is over three thousand years old, shows the harvesting of wheat. Flour from the wheat grains was used to make bread.

Left: Bread was first made by cooking dough on sun-heated stones.

seeds, plants would grow, and they could use the new seeds to make more bread. This discovery soon spread to other Middle Eastern countries and to India and Europe.

When the ancient Egyptians discovered that adding **yeast** to dough before it was cooked made it rise, they began to make softer, lighter bread. The ancient Romans became skilled breadmakers. They ground the seeds, or grains, of cereal plants between heavy round stones, called **millstones,** to make whole-grain flour. They added yeast to their dough, then kneaded it and baked it in clay ovens.

Flour was ground in this way for centuries. In time, wealthy people wanted a lighter, whiter flour. To make it, they **sifted** whole-grain flour through silk sheets to remove the rough pieces. Only the rich could afford bread made from white flour.

Above: The ancient Romans used many different kinds of cereal plants to make a variety of breads.

Right: Breadmakers became more skilled through the ages. This 16th-century picture shows the ovens that were in use and the shape of the loaves that were baked at this time.

Left: The first white flour was made by sifting whole grain flour through sheets of pure silk.

Today, we know that the rough pieces in whole-grain flour are good for us. They contain important ingredients not found in white flour. Because of this, whole-grain bread is popular once more.

9

Bread made from wheat

Wheat flour is made by grinding the grains of wheat plants into a smooth powder.

Some wheat flour is carefully sifted to remove all the **husks,** or outer skins, of the grains. This produces the white flour that is used to make white bread.

Right: Whole wheat bread is made from flour that contains the whole grain of the wheat.

Below: White bread is made from wheat flour that has had the husk of the grain removed.

Wheat flour that has not been treated in this way still has the whole grain of wheat. It makes the brown flour and bread that we call whole grain. This kind of bread contains more of the wheat plant, including the **bran,** or seed coats, and important vitamins.

Wheat is grown in most parts of the world. Huge amounts are grown on the wide, flat plains of Canada and the United States and on the steppes of the Soviet Union.

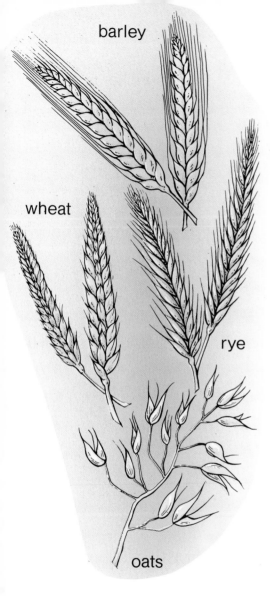

barley

wheat

rye

oats

Leavened and unleavened bread

Bread can be either leavened or unleavened. **Leavened** bread is soft and light. It is made with yeast, which makes the dough rise. **Unleavened** bread does not contain yeast. It is flatter and heavier than leavened bread.

Some flours, such as rye and wheat, contain a great deal of a protein called **gluten.** This protein is useful when making leavened bread. It works with the yeast to make the dough rise.

Rye flour is used to make a very dark leavened

Right: A field of wheat ready for harvesting

12

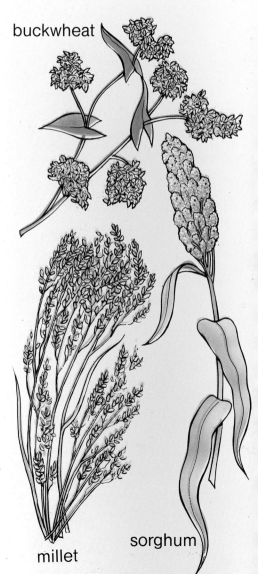

Left: Pumpernickel is a black rye bread.

buckwheat

millet

sorghum

bread called pumpernickel, as well as other breads that are eaten throughout Eastern Europe and Scandinavia.

Flour containing gluten can also be used to make unleavened bread if the yeast is left out of the dough. Chappatis are a kind of unleavened bread made from wheat flour. They are circles of dough that have been rolled out and cooked in oil.

Rye and wheat are just two of the flours that can be used in bread. Bread can also be made from such cereal plants as oats, barley, and buckwheat.

Bread as food

To keep our bodies working well, we need **carbohydrates** and fat to give us energy. We need minerals such as iron, which keeps our blood healthy, and calcium to give us strong bones and teeth. We need vitamin B to help us digest our food and **fiber** to keep our digestive systems working properly. The seeds of cereal plants contain all these good things.

Below: This diagram shows the amount of carbohydrates, moisture, protein, fiber, minerals, vitamin B, and fat in an average loaf of bread.

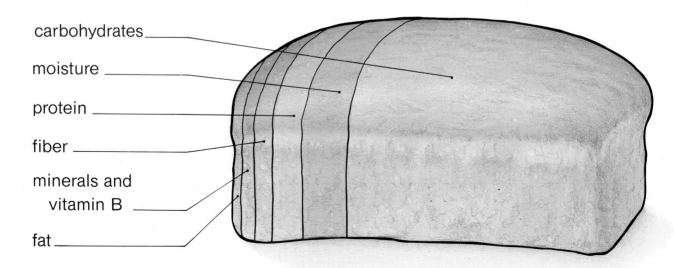

carbohydrates

moisture

protein

fiber

minerals and vitamin B

fat

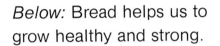

Right: The unleavened bread of Afghanistan

Below: Bread helps us to grow healthy and strong.

Whole-grain flour is much better for us than white flour because it contains all of the healthy ingredients found in cereal plants. Whole-grain flour helps us to stay fit by supplying our bodies with substances we need.

Today, white flour is sometimes **bleached** and has most of the good ingredients taken out of it. Often, vitamins and minerals have to be added to white flour for it to have any real food value at all. Bread is a major part of our daily diet, so it is very important that it be nutritious to help us stay healthy.

Bread from a bakery

Below: These boys from New Caledonia in the South Pacific are carrying freshly baked loaves home from the bakery.

Some people make their own bread at home (you can find out how on pages 26–29). Others buy their bread from a bakery.

Bakeries make their bread fresh every day. First, the correct amount of flour is measured out and put into a large mixing machine. Salt, yeast,

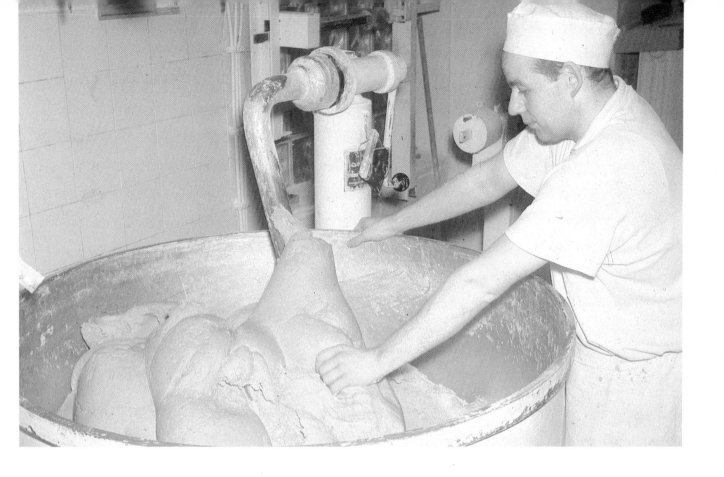

Above: The baker puts the right amount of flour, salt, yeast, fat, and water into this huge bowl, and the dough hook mixes them together.

and a little fat are added, and then the right amount of water is put in. These ingredients are mixed together and kneaded by a **dough hook** inside the machine to make a soft dough. Then the dough is set aside so the yeast can do its work.

Yeast is a member of the fungus family and is

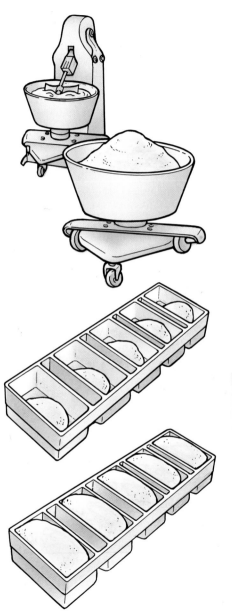

made up of thousands of tiny living cells. They feed on sugar and starch, or carbohydrates, which can be found in bread dough. When the yeast is mixed into the warm, starchy dough, it begins to feed and multiply rapidly. As it grows, it gives off the gas carbon dioxide, which forms bubbles in the dough. The gluten in the flour allows the dough to stretch and rise.

When the dough has risen for the first time, it is kneaded again to get rid of any big air bubbles. Then it is put into pans and left to rise once more.

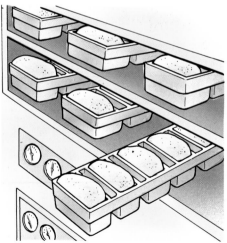

Above: These loaves have been kneaded, left to rise, and shaped. They are now ready to go into the oven to be baked.

The bread is ready to be baked after it has risen a second time. The pans of dough are placed on large trays in a hot oven. The heat cooks the bread and kills off the yeast, leaving air bubbles in the dough that make the loaves soft and light.

When the bread is done, it is taken out of the oven and left to cool. Then it is ready to be sold.

Bread from a factory

Below: This diagram shows the many different stages of breadmaking in a factory.

A lot of small bakeries still make and sell their own bread, but in many countries bread is also produced in huge factories. The breadmaking process in a factory is like that used in bakeries, but almost all the work is done by machines.

The baker's job is to check the bread at each

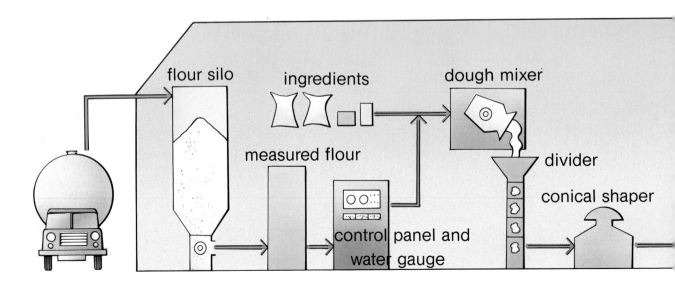

flour silo

ingredients

dough mixer

measured flour

divider

conical shaper

control panel and water gauge

stage as it goes through the machines. Factories can produce loaves much faster than bakeries. The loaves are automatically sliced and wrapped, ready for us to eat. Large trucks deliver the finished bread to supermarkets and stores.

Using huge factories is a cheaper and more efficient way of baking bread, but many people still prefer to buy freshly baked bread from their local bakery.

first rising

dough molder

second rising

oven

delivery to stores

Beliefs about bread

Bread has played an important part in history, so it is not surprising that there are many beliefs about it.

In Muslim countries, bread is traditionally baked for the feast of Id al-Fitr, which follows Ramadan, a month of fasting. Bread is so

Below: In Bahrain, Muslim bakers make vast quantities of bread to eat at the feast of Id al-Fitr.

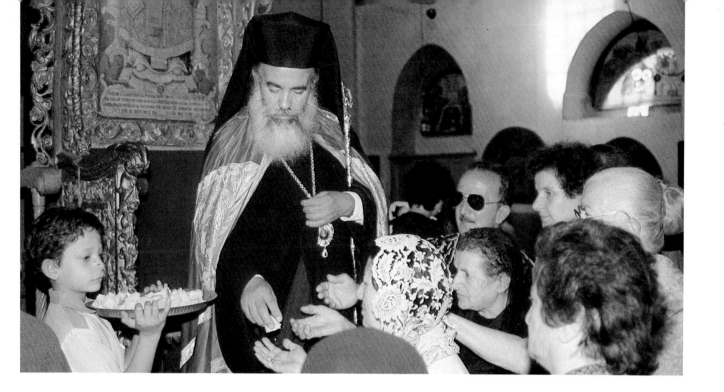

Above: At this Greek Orthodox church, pieces of bread are eaten as part of the Holy Communion ceremony.

important in these countries that the Arabic words for bread and life are almost the same.

In the Christian ceremony of Holy Communion, bread is broken and shared in memory of Christ's Last Supper with his disciples.

Bread also plays an important part in the Jewish religion. On the Sabbath, a blessing is said over two specially baked loaves of bread.

The bread is then eaten as a reminder that God miraculously provided food for the Jews on their journey to the Promised Land.

In the Soviet Union, the word for hospitality means "bread and salt." It is an old custom to give a round, freshly baked loaf of bread to a guest, along with a wooden bowl of salt. This is

Below: Before the Jewish Sabbath meal begins, a blessing is said over two specially baked loaves of bread. They are then cut and eaten with the meal.

Above: A bishop gives bread, as Holy Communion, to the people of the Vai'fa village, Papua New Guinea.

traditionally a sign of honor and respect toward that person.

There are other ceremonies and beliefs involving bread. There are people who believe that bread can keep away illness. In some religions, bread is offered as a sacrifice to a god. Many people consider bread to be so precious that it is a sin to waste it.

A recipe for whole wheat bread

This recipe makes three medium loaves of bread.

You will need:

3 1/3 cups warm water
1 ounce fresh yeast
2 tablespoons brown sugar
10–12 cups whole wheat
flour
1 tablespoon salt
2 tablespoons vegetable oil

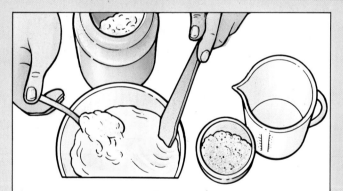

1. Pour the warm water into a large mixing bowl. Add the yeast and sugar. Slowly add enough flour, stirring all the time, to make the dough thick and creamy.

2. Beat the mixture with a large spoon to get as much air into the dough as possible. Cover bowl and leave it in a warm, dry place to rise for 20–30 minutes.

3. Sprinkle the salt over the dough and add the oil. Stir in more flour until the dough forms a ball but is still sticky.

4. Cover your hands and a flat work surface with flour. Knead the dough well, adding flour when it begins to stick to your hands.

5. To knead dough, press it down and away from you with the heels of your hands. Then fold the dough in half by pulling the farthest portion over the nearest. Repeat these steps for 5–10 minutes, adding more flour when necessary.

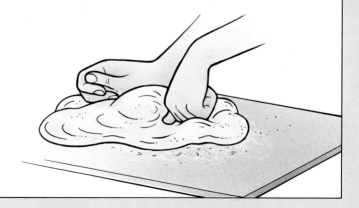

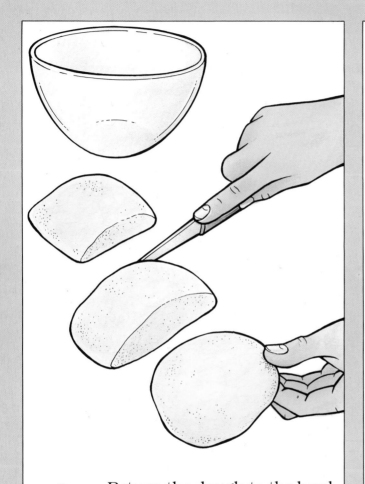

6. Return the dough to the bowl, cover, and leave it to rise for 30 minutes. Separate the dough into three equal pieces, and form them into loaves with your hands.

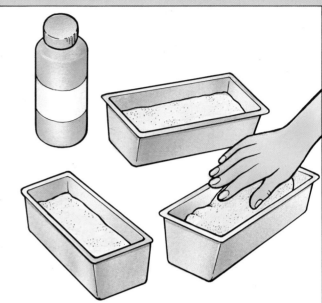

7. Preheat the oven to 425° F. Oil three baking pans and place a loaf in each pan. Bake for 45 minutes. Then take the bread out of the oven and leave it to cool.